WINDOWS OF WORSHIP™

hope

hope

When I'm
COPING WITH LOSS

:: DEVOTIONAL JOURNAL ::

Greg Allen ▪ Rick Rusaw ▪ Dan Stuecher
Paul S. Williams, *Editor*

Standard
PUBLISHING

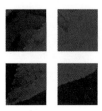

© 2004 CNI Holdings Corp., Windows of Worship is a Trademark of
Christian Network, Inc.

Published by Standard Publishing, Cincinnati, Ohio. A division of Standex
International Corporation. Printed in China.

Cover and interior design by Rule29.

Discover where to watch *Worship* in your town by logging on to
www.Worship.net.

Scripture taken from the HOLY BIBLE, NEW INTERNATIONAL VERSION®. NIV®. Copyright ©
1973, 1978, 1984 by International Bible Society. Used by permission of Zondervan. All rights
reserved.

ISBN 0-7847-1516-5

09 08 07 06 05 04   9 8 7 6 5 4 3 2

We were made to worship...

The first song I remember Grandma Stone singing to me was "Jesus Loves Me." As a three-year-old I sat on her lap on the front porch swing and asked her to sing it over and over again. Before my daughter Jana could speak, she hummed the same tune, its melody unmistakable as she played on the family room floor. We were made to worship.

To worship God is to walk through the shadows into a familiar welcoming place, where the fire never dies and the light is soft and glowing. To worship God is to know we are truly home, acting on a desire deep in our souls. Long before we rationally understand the truth of Christ, we want to praise someone or something for bringing love and beauty, joy and hope into the world.

At the Christian Network, our desire is simple. Whether through the written page or the television screen, we hope these words and images will draw you to worship, as we thank our Creator for breathing life and love into his creation.

Paul S. Williams
Chairman of the Board of Stewards
The Christian Network, Inc.

Suffering with Hope

What you sow does not come to life unless it dies. When you sow, you do not plant the body that will be, but just a seed, perhaps of wheat or of something else. But God gives it a body as he has determined, and to each kind of seed he gives its own body. . . . So will it be with the resurrection of the dead. The body that is sown is perishable, it is raised imperishable; it is sown in dishonor, it is raised in glory; it is sown in weakness, it is raised in power. . . . Listen, I tell you a mystery: We will not all sleep, but we will all be changed—in a flash, in the twinkling of an eye, at the last trumpet. For the trumpet will sound, the dead will be raised imperishable, and we will be changed. For the perishable must clothe itself with the imperishable, and the mortal with immortality.

1 CORINTHIANS 15:36–38, 42, 43, 51–53

SUFFERING WITH HOPE

I am an avid mountain hiker. On several occasions I've climbed to the top of 14,000-foot peaks. I acclimate quickly to the altitude and find the hiking invigorating—to a point. "To a point" because there comes a moment in every trip when climbing isn't fun anymore; too many switchbacks on too many trails, too much wind and cold. At those moments the only thing that keeps me going is the knowledge of the incredible feeling I'll have when I get to the top.

But on more than one occasion, I've gotten within a few hundred feet of the top and been turned back by bad weather. And then, the trip down is pure drudgery. Climbing without purpose, it feels like. I've just spent hours on the mountain with nothing to show for it.

6

It's one thing to have a day of hiking spoiled. It's another when your whole life feels like one long, winding, cold, windswept trail to nowhere. Viktor Frankl, survivor of a Nazi concentration camp, expressed well one of the greatest fears of those who suffer. "Despair," he said, "is suffering without meaning."

Most of us see only the negative side to suffering. It's an interruption of pursuing what we want to pursue. We try to ignore long-term suffering and the reality of death. But in the process, we're missing something. There will come a time when most of us will suffer. We will not get well. The only end to our suffering will be death itself. And what do we do then?

When the English poet John Donne was deathly ill, sure he would soon die, he wondered if the church bells he heard were tolling for him. That is when he wrote, "If a clod be washed away by the sea, Europe is the less. . . . Any man's death diminishes me, because I am involved in mankind, and therefore never send to know for whom the bell tolls; it tolls for thee."

We are all a part of one another's suffering. With every death we are aware of our deep connectedness to others. With every death we feel a part of ourselves has been ripped from us. Donne had it right. Every man's death diminishes me, because none of us were made for this. Death and suffering are aliens that should be fought with great devotion. They are our enemies, all. Unless . . .

Suppose suffering unto death prepared us for something greater. Suppose it prepared us for a mountaintop like none we had envisioned before. Suppose that which ends life also opens a door to a new life. We don't think much about Heaven nowadays. The notion seems quaint, old-fashioned, outdated. But when we leave out Heaven, we leave out hope. Suffering and death are real. They can't be avoided forever. But the good news is that Heaven is real too.

7

After living through his horrible illness, John Donne never feared death again, because he had finally come to realize that death was not the final word:

> Death be not proud though some have called thee
> Mighty and dreadful, for thou art not so . . .
> One short sleep past, we wake eternally,
> And death shall be no more; death, thou shalt die.

—Paul S. Williams

Think of times in the past when you have suffered or struggled to reach something wonderful. (Perhaps you endured pregnancy and labor to have a child, you worked through exhaustion and frustration to finish a project, or you struggled through dark times with a loved one and saw him or her come out victorious.) Write about that experience—your feelings, how God helped you, and what you learned.

_____

_____

_____

_____

_____

_____

_____

_____

_____

_____

_____

Are you facing suffering right now? Meditate on the passages from 1 Corinthians and write out your impressions and feelings. How does the hope of an immortal body and of Heaven put a new light on your suffering?

_____

_____

_____

_____

_____

_____

_____

_____

_____

_____

_____

_____

Good Friday Too!

The soldiers led Jesus away. . . . They put a purple robe on him,
then twisted together a crown of thorns and set it on him. And
they began to call out to him, "Hail, king of the Jews!" Again and
again they struck him on the head with a staff and spit on him.
Falling on their knees, they paid homage to him. And when they
had mocked him, they took off the purple robe and put his own
clothes on him. . . . They brought Jesus to the place called
Golgotha (which means The Place of the Skull). . . . And they
crucified him. Dividing up his clothes, they cast lots to see what
each would get. . . . At the sixth hour darkness came over the
whole land until the ninth hour. And at the ninth hour Jesus
cried out in a loud voice, "Eloi, Eloi, lama sabachthani?"—
which means, "My God, my God, why have you forsaken me?" . . .
With a loud cry, Jesus breathed his last.

MARK 15:16–20, 22, 24, 33, 34, 37

GOOD FRIDAY TOO!

When I was a child I understood God as a swashbuckling hero, strong, powerful, and confident. An "in control" God who looked a lot like the Lone Ranger.

When I read the words Jesus spoke on the cross, "My God, my God, why have you forsaken me?" I didn't get it. That didn't seem like something the Lone Ranger would say. I had a hard time putting my arms around a suffering Christ, one who might actually have felt forsaken by his Father.

But that was before life knocked me around a good bit. Before I so clearly encountered my own weaknesses. Before I came to understand there will always be confusion on this side of eternity. And slowly, I began to appreciate the God who felt forsaken.

My daughter, Jael, came home from college one semester with a gold cross necklace. Jesus was still on the cross. My wife commented, "Why do you have a necklace with Jesus still on the cross? I like empty crosses better. They're a better symbol of the resurrection."

I thought about it for a few minutes, and then spoke up in sup-
port of Jael and her cross necklace. "This necklace shows the
suffering Jesus," I said. "The one in agony. The one at the end
of his rope. I understand that Jesus. I identify with that Jesus.
I like the necklace." My daughter grinned. My wife looked
thoughtful. I just held the cross in my hand and ran my fingers
across the outline of Jesus hanging there.

If Jesus did, in fact, feel abandoned by his Father, then he's
a man I can trust. He is someone who knows how I feel during
the long dark nights. He is not the conquering hero, riding in
with a sword and a strong word, but the wounded healer, full of
compassion and understanding. The one who knows suffering
before he knows hope.

I can identify with that Jesus. Yes, Christianity is about the resurrection, and yes, we should celebrate Easter, make no mistake
about it. But let's not forget about Good Friday too.

—Paul S. Williams

Write about the thoughts and feelings you have as you read the account of Jesus' death. What does it mean to you to know that he suffered and felt abandoned, just as you do sometimes?

Write out a prayer, telling God about your suffering. Ask him for renewed hope and thank him for the fact that he truly understands because he suffered too.

_____

_____

_____

_____

_____

_____

_____

_____

_____

_____

_____

_____

_____

Requiem

The Father . . . has qualified you to share in the inheritance of the
saints in the kingdom of light. For he has rescued us from the
dominion of darkness and brought us into the kingdom of the Son
he loves.

COLOSSIANS 1:12, 13

REQUIEM

Have you ever wished you could go back and relive some moment in your past because you know you would appreciate it more now? I'll tell you about one of those experiences for me. I was a senior in high school and had been awarded the honor of participating in a statewide chorus and orchestra event in Louisville, Kentucky. The music program would be performed under the baton of none other than the world famous conductor, Robert Shaw. Only now can I appreciate what a great experience that was. I certainly didn't then.

One of the music selections performed by our chorus was the fourth movement of the German *Requiem* by Johannes Brahms. Even at the time I thought it was some of the most moving music I'd ever heard; but it has only been in my adult life that I've come to learn the story behind it and to appreciate its beauty and penetrating power.

The German composer Johannes Brahms had watched his mentor and friend, Robert Schumann, wither and die from confusion, depression, and anxiety. Brahms would spend years dealing with the heartbreak of that loss. Just a few years later his mother would die and his grief would be rekindled. Brahms cherished his mother with a deeper affection than he held for any other member of his family, and her death left him with a sense of abandonment.

His grief though, would express itself in music, and we should be very grateful it did. For some time, ideas had been forming in his mind for a requiem, or mass for the dead.

Brahms would disregard convention and compose his requiem to be performed not only in the church but in secular venues as well. He would studiously work to convey his conviction that death was something to be understood as a central problem of all human existence. He chose his own biblical passages from Martin Luther's translation of Scripture instead of those prescribed by the Catholic Church, a highly unconventional approach for his day. When the first three movements of the German *Requiem* by Johannes Brahms were premiered in Vienna on December 1, 1867, there were times when the audience booed and hissed. Not exactly what a composer wants to hear in reaction to his music!

Undaunted, Brahms set to work and finished the requiem. The completed work was performed in its entirety two years later in Leipzig, Germany. It was the greatest musical triumph of his life. The audience reaction to the music was overwhelming. The *Requiem* would be performed throughout Germany over 20 times in the following year alone, and it is still revered today.

Why the stark difference in reaction to the two performances? The first three movements of the unfinished work performed in Vienna focused on the pain and finality of death. The last three movements added to the performance in Leipzig powerfully declared our victory over death, the beauty of God's dwelling place and the joy we will experience in being united with those who have gone before us. One performance conveyed despair, the other hope; one spoke of defeat while the other declared victory; the first grieved over separation while the second celebrated reunion. No wonder the difference in response!

The heartache and separation of death are very real but only part of the reality. Stop there and it will most certainly be the source of despair, even terror. Like the Viennese audience, we are repelled by it. But through the resurrection of Jesus Christ, God has conquered death and made a way for us to follow him into eternal life. That part of God's composition is worthy of a standing ovation indeed!

—*Dan Stuecher*

When you think about death, especially the deaths of those you
love the most, what are your first thoughts and feelings?

20

_____

_____

_____

_____

_____

_____

_____

_____

_____

_____

_____

_____

_____

_____

Now think about the fact that death isn't the end for those who know Jesus. How does this change your thoughts and feelings?

_____

_____

_____

_____

_____

_____

_____

_____

_____

_____

_____

_____

_____

Bear Stickers!

Have mercy on me, O God,

    according to your unfailing love;

according to your great compassion

    blot out my transgressions.

Wash away all my iniquity

    and cleanse me from my sin.

For I know my transgressions,

    and my sin is always before me. . . .

Create in me a pure heart, O God,

    and renew a steadfast spirit within me.

Do not cast me from your presence

    or take your Holy Spirit from me.

Restore to me the joy of your salvation

    and grant me a willing spirit, to sustain me.

PSALM 51:1–3, 10–12

BEAR STICKERS!

He was running a little late for lunch and I was afraid he wouldn't show—afraid he'd changed his mind and decided not to get together after all. It had been a long time since he had moved to a southern state. He had come to heal, repair relationships, and be reconciled to his calling.

His work had been greatly admired. With strong leadership skills and a national presence, he had spoken several times at the college I attended, and I was always moved by his words. Unfortunately, however, his life came crashing down as a result of his own bad decisions. He lost his job, his influence, his friends, and he just about lost his family. In failure and shame, he moved south.

I was looking forward to our lunch together. When my friend arrived at the restaurant, he was carrying a small display case. We talked about the weather and ordered lunch. Then he shared the ache of his heart in the aftermath of his poor choices. He challenged me to be smart, to watch my steps, and to be careful of my vulnerabilities—lessons he had learned all too painfully.

As we finished lunch, he opened his display case and offered me some little bear stickers for my children—the kind a teacher puts on a student's homework paper. That's right. This once nationally known ministry leader was now reduced to selling small promotional items for corporations: pencils, calendars, tiny calculators, and yes, bear stickers. As he closed his case and headed out to make another sale, I was overwhelmed by the sadness of it all. There is a consequence to bad decisions.

My children put one of those stickers on my travel alarm. I don't know why they put it there, but they did. And for years, it stayed on that alarm as a reminder. A reminder of how quickly a broken promise can ruin your entire life. Every time I look at that sticker I think of the childhood story of Humpty Dumpty. Sometimes even all the king's horses and all the king's men can't put one's character together again. Some bad decisions stay with us for a very long time.

But there is good news in this story. It is now years later, and my friend is back in ministry again. I've seen him plenty of times since that lunch. He is preaching again. He is growing in grace, and he hasn't sold a bear sticker in a long, long time. With a humble spirit and great wisdom, he knows some very good news. He knows there is someone who does put back together the most broken of pieces and mends the most wounded of hearts.

—Rick Rusaw

25

What are some mistakes you've made in your life that you truly regret? Are there things you've done that still make you feel terrible to think about them? Are you still facing the consequences of those mistakes? Take some time to write out those regrets here.

Now, take those regrets and mistakes to God in prayer. Write out all your feelings about them and ask for forgiveness for each one, remembering that God is ready and willing to restore and heal you.

Hope for a New Tent

*We groan, longing to be clothed with our heavenly dwelling,
because when we are clothed, we will not be found naked.
For while we are in this tent, we groan and are burdened,
because we do not wish to be unclothed but to be clothed with our
heavenly dwelling, so that what is mortal may be swallowed up
by life. Now it is God who has made us for this very purpose and
has given us the Spirit as a deposit, guaranteeing what is to come.
Therefore we are always confident and know that as long as we
are at home in the body we are away from the Lord.*

2 corinthians 5:2–6

HOPE FOR A NEW TENT

Heather was accidentally run over by her mom when she was two and has had over 150 major surgeries in 30 years of life. Heather's mom, Sandy, has multiple sclerosis, which forces her to walk with a cane. She also has a brain tumor that occasionally leaves her blind.

Near the time of the accident, Sandy and Heather watched their apartment building burn to the ground. Following Sandy's divorce, finances got so tough that they didn't have much to eat. A daughter with severe, multiple injuries, a mom with MS, no husband, and no money. Wow! Are you depressed yet? Are you wondering, "Where is the hope in this story?"

Sandy and Heather both have looked death square in the face . . . and smiled. Even in the midst of their terrible suffering they have not given up on life. To the contrary, Sandy and Heather have more "fight" than most of us. You see, there is a reason for their hope.

Sandy and Heather fight MS, tumors, and surgeries every day, but they have not conceded to the Grim Reaper. The reason they are so full of life is that they are not afraid of death. And they don't even complain about their physical bodies because they know they have the hope of a new tent. A new what? A new tent.

The apostle Paul wanted to encourage people who struggled with the same enemies we fight today—disease, deformity, and death. Like Sandy and Heather, the early Christians wondered if there was hope for their bodies to get better. Paul wrote a letter and told them, "Now we know that if the earthly tent we live in is destroyed, we have a building from God, an eternal house in heaven, not built with human hands." In other words, life here is temporary, these bodies were not meant to last forever. But our bodies in Heaven, they are for eternity.

There are plenty of times in the Bible where people faced unbelievable suffering. The apostle Paul spoke to those people, and to Sandy and Heather, and even to you and me when he spoke these words from 2 Corinthians 4:16–18: "We do not lose heart. Though outwardly we are wasting away, yet inwardly we are being renewed day by day. For our light and momentary troubles are achieving for us an eternal glory that far outweighs them all. So we fix our eyes not on what is seen, but on what is unseen. For what is seen is temporary, but what is unseen is eternal."

—*Greg Allen*

What physical struggles are you dealing with right now that make you long for your new body in Heaven? What is most frustrating about these struggles?

_____

_____

_____

_____

_____

_____

_____

_____

_____

_____

_____

_____

_____

_____

Take each physical ailment you or someone you love deals with and write them out. Beside each one write an activity you would do if that ailment was healed. (For example, if you have foot problems you might write that you'd take long walks if you could.) When you finish, say a prayer, thanking the Lord that one day, even if it is in Heaven, he will heal you and you'll be able to do all those things you long to do!

_____

_____

_____

_____

_____

_____

_____

_____

_____

_____

_____

Scared of the Dark

Jesus . . . said, "I am the light of the world. Whoever follows me

will never walk in darkness, but will have the light of life."

JOHN 8:12

SCARED OF THE DARK

When I was a little boy I enjoyed a family tradition of eating popcorn and playing cards with my parents just before bedtime. The next part of the tradition I didn't enjoy so much. Mom and Dad would say, "OK, Greg, it's time for bed, don't forget to brush your teeth." I didn't mind brushing my teeth, but I was scared to go to bed. When I got to my bedroom I'd pull back the covers and go to the light switch. Then I would turn it off, run to my bed, and pull the covers over my head. I can remember being so hot I felt as if I'd suffocate, but I wouldn't move those sheets. Why? I was afraid of the dark.

What was it about the dark that frightened me so? I think I was afraid of being alone.

As a little boy I thrived on being with people. For that matter, I thrive on it now. As an adult I have learned to enjoy solitude, but 35 years ago it was traumatic. It is for most children. We're nurtured and cared for by our parents and we know quite well that we're not ready to tackle the world alone. But somewhere deep inside we know that we entered this world alone, and we will leave it that way. And as a child, that is a thing to fear. But as we grow older, there is a way to feel safe and secure, even when we are alone.

For many people, the fear of being alone never really leaves. It is very real. But at some point we must confront that childhood fear. We must acknowledge the reality that, yes, we do enter this world alone and we will leave it that way too. That is, unless there is a loving God who came to Earth as a man and defeated the ultimate "aloneness" called death. And then promised to send his Spirit as a comforter, a guide, a companion who will never leave us or forsake us. If that were true, then we never would be alone, would we? Not ever!

—*Greg Allen*

What did you fear as a child? Do you still fear the same things?
Why or why not?

_____

_____

_____

_____

_____

_____

_____

_____

_____

_____

_____

_____

_____

What do you fear the most now? Why?

_____

_____

_____

_____

_____

_____

_____

_____

_____

_____

_____

_____

_____

_____

Write a prayer offering all your fears and worries up to the Lord.
Ask him to give you courage to face them and the reminder of
his presence even in dark times.

_____

_____

_____

_____

_____

_____

_____

_____

_____

_____

_____

_____

_____

Full Steam Ahead

We rejoice in the hope of the glory of God. Not only so, but we also rejoice in our sufferings, because we know that suffering produces perseverance; perseverance, character; and character, hope.

ROMANS 5:2–4

FULL STEAM AHEAD

John Fitch sold 150 acres of land to an innkeeper. In return, the innkeeper agreed to give Fitch a pint of whiskey a day until Fitch drank himself to death. When it didn't work fast enough, Fitch sold the man more land so he could double his daily dose of whiskey. Death still came too slowly, so in 1798 a bottle of opium pills fulfilled John Fitch's wish.

You probably never heard of John Fitch, but he likely invented the first steamboat. Most people think it was Robert Fulton, but Fitch had already logged over 2,000 miles traveling between Philadelphia and Trenton, New Jersey, on a steamboat he built about 20 years before Fulton's famous voyage on the *Clermont.* So how did a brilliant man like Fitch come to such a terrible end? What was it that Fulton had that John Fitch didn't have? It wasn't intelligence. Fitch was extremely bright and obsessed with learning. It wasn't funding. Fitch had managed to secure private financing for his work. And it wasn't a lack of challenges. Both Fulton and Fitch suffered many setbacks.

John Fitch stumbled his way to the bottom of a bottle of pills because of one very important thing that he lost somewhere along the way. Whether traveling by steamship or space shuttle, it's impossible for a man or woman to get anywhere without it. It's not money or intelligence. It's hope! And it's as necessary today as it was in 1798.

A rack of steam-driven canoe paddles drove John Fitch's boat. Most people thought it looked funny, so it never caught on. Robert Fulton learned from Fitch's mistakes as well as his own. He too endured a lot of humiliation, but he kept at it until he perfected the *Clermont*. And so it is Fulton whom history remembers. It wasn't money, intelligence, or hard work that separated his success from John Fitch's tragic end. What separated these two men was one simple thing—hope.

Hope inspires endurance. Hope gives us the will go to on. Hope that, in spite of our humiliation, our setbacks, and our frustrations, we will prevail. If we will keep our faces turned steadfastly to what is true, our creativity engaged, and our hearts full of hope, we can build our own *Clermont*.

—Eric Snyder for Rick Rusaw

43

What dreams have you seen come true so far in your life? What dreams have you pursued that have so far met with failure?

How will you go about continuing to pursue those dreams that have failed? How will you hold on to hope as you go forward?

_____

_____

_____

_____

_____

_____

45

_____

_____

_____

_____

_____

_____

_____

_____

One Little Word

Who shall separate us from the love of Christ? Shall trouble or hardship or persecution or famine or nakedness or danger or sword? . . . No, in all these things we are more than conquerors through him who loved us. For I am convinced that neither death nor life, neither angels nor demons, neither the present nor the future, nor any powers, neither height nor depth, nor anything else in all creation, will be able to separate us from the love of God that is in Christ Jesus our Lord.

ROMANS 8:35, 37–39

ONE LITTLE WORD

For most of my life I've been fortunate to look only from a distance on places where great evil was done. I've never visited the concentration camps in Germany or the killing fields of Cambodia. But in September of 2001 I drove from my Long Island home into New York City and saw a scene of devastation I could never have imagined. Television is good at some things. Showing the magnitude of destruction at the World Trade Center in Manhattan is not one of them.

A week after the September 11 tragedy I began working to distribute over a million dollars in relief funds through churches in the New York area. Since we were giving the funds through churches we had planted, we had no difficulty identifying needs and meeting them quickly. But within a couple of weeks I was weary. I had seen too much sadness in too many families. My spirits were sinking fast. One warm September afternoon I decided to take a break and go out for a long run along the Great South Bay on Long Island's south shore. What happened next renewed my soul.

I ran beside the cool waters and watched the blue-gray waves blend with the fall sky. I passed marshlands and wind-shaped evergreens and watched mallards fly overhead. It was good to be touched by beauty, peace, and tranquility.

The coastline was beautiful, but an even more precious sight greeted me as I arrived home. Many young families have moved into our neighborhood over the past few years. I had noticed one house in particular. A young couple had done a beautiful job renovating their new home. A couple of years ago I noticed a plywood stork in the front lawn announcing the birth of a firstborn son, Kyle. In late August of 2001, another stork announced the arrival of a daughter, Camryn Marie.

As I ran back home that warm September afternoon, I came upon Camryn Marie out taking a stroller ride with Mom, Dad, and big brother Kyle. Mom and Dad are a good-looking young couple, fit and healthy. As I ran past them, I said to Camryn's mother, "Congratulations." She replied with a quick "thank you." Before I could even turn the corner, my eyes filled with tears. Not just a rogue tear or two—tears streamed down my cheeks until I could barely see.

I don't know Camryn's mother and father very well. At that point we had never spoken. But something reached out and grabbed me by the heart that afternoon.

In the midst of all the evil, tragedy, and death of that September, here was a beautiful family out for an afternoon stroll. I had seen so much death and destruction and despair, but here was life and love and wholeness. And at that moment I remembered what I hadn't taken hold of since the terrible events of September 11. No matter how hard evil tries, love wins every time. The beauty of one, loving, young family out for an afternoon stroll is a far more powerful image than all the havoc evil can wreak across the entire globe.

49

And as I wiped the tears from my eyes, my mind went back to the words of a powerful old hymn we sang at church on the Sunday after the attacks: "And though this world, with devils filled, should threaten to undo us, we will not fear, for God hath willed His truth to triumph through us. The prince of darkness grim, we tremble not for him—his rage we can endure, for lo, his doom is sure: one little word shall fell him."

As I watched Camryn Marie, Kyle, and their mom and dad lovingly taking their stroll on that warm fall day, I remembered one little word that defeats all evil.

That word is love.

—Paul S. Williams

List several specific things, either large or small, that have
caused you sorrow in your life.

_____

_____

_____

_____

_____

_____

_____

_____

_____

_____

_____

_____

_____

Now, list all the specific things, large and small, that bring joy, love, and hope to your life. Thank the Lord for the love he shows us each day through these things.

David and Goliath

I can do everything through him who gives me strength.

PHILIPPIANS 4:13

DAVID AND GOLIATH

I could see it in her eyes. I could hear it in her voice. Hope. I could see and hear hope. Laura Blakemore, a 13-year-old middle school student, was speaking to about 2,500 people at youth night at church. We had to watch and listen to Laura on video because she was in the hospital. You see, Laura is dealing with cancer.

But she was smiling, even laughing. You could see the hope in Laura's smile, and hear it in her laugh. And even though Laura was just a little girl facing a big disease, she wasn't afraid. Why? Why does a middle school girl have joy in spite of an intruding enemy like cancer? As we listened to Laura talk that night it became clear that her faith in God brought her hope. Her hope was not so much that her cancer would be healed for this life, but that God had a perfect body waiting for her in the next.

54

Laura has hope for her future. Cancer may destroy her body on Earth, but she has faith that God will restore her body in Heaven. And what thrills me about Laura is her joy and trust in God even while facing the giant of cancer.

You've heard about David and the giant in his life—a 9-foot-tall enemy warrior named Goliath. It's possible that David wasn't much older than Laura. It's certain that Goliath was a giant of a man and a seasoned warrior. And like Laura's battle with cancer, nobody wanted to fight Goliath because they didn't see much hope for victory. Nobody, that is, except for a boy named David. That young man stood in the face of the 9-foot giant and told him that he came in the name of God. David then took a stone and slung it toward Goliath, a stone that struck dead center on his forehead and killed him. But it wasn't the stone and slingshot that really slew Goliath—it was David's trust in God.

First Samuel 17:45 reads like this: "David said to the Philistine, 'You come against me with sword and spear and javelin, but I come against you in the name of the LORD Almighty." The boy David and the girl Laura had more hope in God than in weapons and medicine. Hope in God may not always kill 9-foot giants or cure cancer in this life, but hope in God will enable us to see the joy of living even in the face of death.

The way Laura Blakemore is dealing with her cancer and the way David dealt with Goliath remind me how much easier it is for me to put my hope in the things I see, like radiation and chemo for cancer, or a weapon to use when fighting a 9-foot giant. But the Bible encourages me to place my hope in what I can't see. The Bible encourages us all to fix our eyes on God—the ultimate source of hope.

—*Greg Allen*

What are the "giants" in your life? How are you fighting them?

_____

_____

_____

_____

_____

_____

_____

_____

_____

_____

_____

_____

_____

_____

_____

Write a prayer asking God for his strength and his weapons to defeat the "giants" of this world. He will be faithful to arm you!

_____

_____

_____

_____

_____

_____

57

_____

_____

_____

_____

_____

_____

_____

_____

Longing

As the deer pants for streams of water,

so my soul pants for you, O God.

My soul thirsts for God, for the living God.

When can I go and meet with God?

PSALM 42:1, 2

LONGING

By 4:00 in the afternoon the freezing March day had just about run its course. The street lamps and the candles from thousands of rooms in the city of Vienna had already begun to illuminate the freshly fallen snow. In a small, second-story room near the old city walls the great composer, Beethoven, lay dying. His life had also all but run its course. Surrounded by books, manuscripts, and music scores, he could see his prized mahogany piano, undoubtedly realizing he would never play it again. The weather grew worse—the wind blew and the snow pelted windows. Suddenly, on that raw winter day, there was a loud clap of thunder accompanied by a bolt of lightning. Opening his eyes Beethoven raised his right hand, and with his fist clenched, he looked upward for several seconds . . . and died.

60

I've stood in the room where Beethoven died. It would be difficult to describe the experience. I have loved his music for too many years to count, so to find myself standing in the very room where he passed from this life defies description. It was much the same sensation as standing on the spot where Lincoln delivered the Gettysburg Address, looking into the workshop of Thomas Edison or gazing on the statue of David sculpted by the hands of Michelangelo. You can name your own spots. For me these places always bring goosebumps, reverence, awe. Why do such feelings arise?

I think it is longing. It is a longing in our minds and hearts for connection to what we consider greatness; a longing for the validation of what we believe. It is a longing to somehow share a moment with our heroes, to hear the actual sound of their voices, to see them from 360 degrees instead of two-dimensional photographs or paintings. It is a longing to know them and be known by them.

One such experience is very much within our grasp.

I can't go to the place where this man was born. Nobody knows exactly where it is. I can't go to the place where he died. Nobody knows where that is for sure, either. I can't enter a house where he lived. I can't step inside a fishing boat he used on occasion. I can't look at any of his clothing under glass in a museum. There are no strands of his hair pressed between the pages of a book. No documents have ever been discovered bearing his handwriting. There are no recordings of his voice and there are no photographs taken of his likeness. I have not one single point of physical contact to satisfy my longing to make connection with the greatest hero of my life. But then, I really don't need to connect to some object from his past, because my hero is alive today. Jesus defeated death. And all I need to do is accept his promise that he is living in me. That is more than enough to satisfy my longing.

—Dan Stuecher

What do you long for? Money? Love? Acceptance? Beauty? List some of your deepest desires.

Do you long for God? For a relationship with Jesus? How might knowing God fulfill your longings?

_____

_____

_____

_____

_____

_____

63

_____

_____

_____

_____

_____

_____

_____

_____

O Death, Where Is Your Sting?

When the perishable has been clothed with the imperishable,

and the mortal with immortality, then the saying that is written

will come true: "Death has been swallowed up in victory."

"Where, O death, is your victory?

Where, O death, is your sting?"

1 CORINTHIANS 15:54, 55

O DEATH, WHERE IS YOUR STING?

For reasons I still don't fully understand, I spent a lot of time thinking about death and Heaven when I was in my twenties. No one close to me had died. I have no idea why I thought so much about death. But I do know that at that young age I was very confident of Heaven. Sure of it. I used to tell my friends that when I died I was going to have someone put a tape recorder behind my casket that played my voice saying, "Hey, glad you came, but I'm not here. I'm dancing around Heaven looking up old relatives and going fishing with my grandfather."

By the time I was 30, though, I didn't think much about Heaven anymore. I was busy raising a family and building a career. Besides, I lived in the Northeast, where discussion of Heaven is best left out of polite conversation, lest you be seen as a religious fanatic. And so I just quit thinking about death or Heaven. I was very busy focusing on this life.

But then my forties arrived. Not a particularly fun decade. I found myself thinking a lot about death, but not much about Heaven. It seemed too elusive to contemplate while life was beating me up on Earth. I was just trying to get from one day to the next. I had no energy to think about anything else.

Frederick Buechner said he once would have jumped at the chance to live forever. But now that he is in his seventies, he's no longer enamored by that idea. He says if it's true that you're never happier than your most unhappy child, just think about how tough life would be if you had hundreds of future generations to worry about. No, he decided he'd have to pass on living in this world forever.

This life does wear me out. I get tired. And I'm starting to see the end of life as something other than a dreadful enemy. Moving on doesn't seem like such a bad idea anymore.

In my twenties I thought a lot about Heaven. And now, 30 years later, I think a lot about it again. I'm wiser now. Less naïve. Hopefully more mature. Now I think of Heaven as a place where I'll work out all the stuff I never figured out in this life. And work it out in a way that always proves redemptive.

The words of poet T.S. Eliot come to mind: "Old men ought to be explorers. Here and there does not matter. We must be still and still moving into another intensity for a further union, a deeper communion through the dark cold and the empty desolation. The waves cry, the wind cries, the vast waters of the petrel and the porpoise. In my end is my beginning."

—Paul S. Williams

What are your thoughts and feelings about Heaven? Why do you think you feel the way you do?

_____

_____

_____

_____

_____

_____

_____

_____

_____

_____

_____

_____

Read the descriptions of Heaven in Revelation 21 and 22. How does this picture of Heaven take the "sting" out of death for you?

_____

_____

_____

_____

_____

_____

_____

69

_____

_____

_____

_____

_____

_____

_____

_____

Mother's Day

The LORD is close to the brokenhearted

and saves those who are crushed in spirit.

PSALM 34:18

MOTHER'S DAY

Her name is Pam; she's the mom. His name was Justin, and he
was the son—16 years old and looking forward to his senior year
in high school. It was a typical Saturday morning when Justin
left for his part-time job. About an hour later there was a knock
at the door. Pam answered the front door expecting one of
Justin's friends, but she was surprised to see a police officer.
It was the news every parent hopes never to hear. Justin had just
been killed in a tragic car accident.

There is nothing to say. Words haven't been created to help a
parent grieving the death of a child. Special days intensify the
hurt: Justin's birthday, Thanksgiving, Christmas. But it's
Mother's Day that most seems to pour salt in the wound of
Justin's death. And it keeps coming and coming and coming,
once a year. Each May Pam is reminded that the privilege of
raising her son was limited to 16 years. We should all remember
that moms who have lost children still have to face Mother's Day.

Jane is the mom of three daughters, so you'd think that Mother's
Day would be triple fun for her—but it's not. One of Jane's girls,
Marci, has chosen to reject the values she learned from loving
parents. As a matter of fact, Marci is very stubborn. She loves
her mom, but she loves her freedom to choose even more.

Jane still celebrates Mother's Day. Two daughters celebrate their mom's sacrifice and devotion. But the pain and sorrow Jane feels over Marci is felt every day.

Mother's Day is a day of marvelous celebration. It is also a day for prayer—prayer for reconciliation, prayer for peace, prayer for a daughter to return, prayer for healing over a son who can never return.

Mother's Day isn't always a lunch on Sunday accompanied by a well-worded card and a gift certificate to mom's favorite store. Often Mother's Day comes with pain. So why would I share such sad stories about Mother's Day? To remind us that there are moms who hurt, who have lost children, and who are waiting for children to come home. To remind us to pray. Pray that these moms know we still care; pray that God's spirit brings them peace and comfort in the midst of difficult times; and pray that we might be able ease their pain, especially on Mother's Day.

—Greg Allen

Write a prayer for your own mother, or a mother you know, asking for God's blessing upon her today. Then send her a note or give her a call and let her know you prayed for her.

_____

_____

_____

_____

_____

_____

_____

_____

_____

_____

_____

_____

Write a prayer asking God to heal your hurts today. He wants to comfort you no matter who you are.

Road to Emmaus

He [Jesus] said to them, "This is what I told you while I was still with you: Everything must be fulfilled that is written about me in the Law of Moses, the Prophets and the Psalms." Then he opened their minds so they could understand the Scriptures. He told them, "This is what is written: The Christ will suffer and rise from the dead on the third day, and repentance and forgiveness of sins will be preached in his name to all nations, beginning at Jerusalem. You are witnesses of these things. I am going to send you what my Father has promised."

LUKE 24:44–49

ROAD TO EMMAUS

They thought the story would have a different ending. They thought their hopes and dreams would now be realized. But stories often take unusual turns, and it isn't uncommon for hopes and dreams to be dashed. The week had begun with such promise; now they were shuffling home tired, confused, and wondering what had gone wrong. That is, until they met this stranger who seemed to have no idea what had happened. But how could that be? After all, the most widely known person in the world had just been put to death in a horrific public execution. How could this stranger not have known? It was the topic on everyone's lips.

"What are you talking about?" the stranger asked, as he met two men on the road to Emmaus. They were surprised by his question, but they told him the story. "We knew this man who became our friend," they said. "He was a gifted teacher and did some amazing things. We believed him to be the Messiah, our Savior, the one we had hoped would redeem Israel. But our rulers in their jealousy had him put to death, and now it has been three days since he died. Things haven't gone at all like we thought." The stranger challenged them. He said the way things were turning out was, in fact, what the Scriptures taught about the Messiah.

They suddenly realized that they had arrived back home in Emmaus. The stranger was ready to continue on his journey. But something about him made it difficult for them to bid him farewell, so they invited him to dinner. When the stranger broke the bread and prayed the blessing at their humble table they realized "the stranger" was the resurrected Jesus, the Messiah! But as soon as they realized who he was, he was gone.

Now they had a whole new dilemma. Once they had believed in a Messiah who would defeat the political enemies and grant them power. Now they were greeted instead by a Messiah who wandered dusty roads and then disappeared from view.

The ending to a story isn't always what we anticipate. Many an author has left the very best part for the end, and you didn't see the twist in the plot coming. That is how the author of life has chosen to write the story. What seemed like bad news ended up being wonderful news! What seemed like the end was only the beginning. Jesus' death and crucifixion weren't the end of the story; it wasn't the death of hope and dreams. It was in fact the prelude to the story of resurrection that can be written on every heart. Two men who shuffled toward home with heads and hearts heavy met a stranger who was their friend—Jesus resurrected from the dead. And it is this same stranger who can be your friend. He can bring hope to your story and joy to your journey.

—*Paul S. Williams*

Have you had a "story" in your life end differently than you
expected it to? Did this "plot twist" end up being better or worse
than the ending you expected?

_____

_____

_____

_____

_____

_____

_____

_____

_____

_____

_____

_____

_____

No matter what twists and turns your life story takes, Jesus wants to walk through them all with you. Write a prayer, asking for his guidance and presence through the specific "stories" you are living right now.

_____

_____

_____

_____

_____

_____

_____

_____

_____

_____

_____

_____

My Sister's Grave

*I heard a loud voice from the throne saying, "Now the dwelling of
God is with men, and he will live with them. They will be his people, and God himself will be with them and be their God. He will
wipe every tear from their eyes. There will be no more death or
mourning or crying or pain, for the old order of things has passed
away." He who was seated on the throne said, "I am making
everything new!"*

REVELATION 21:3–5

MY SISTER'S GRAVE

It may seem strange, but I like going to my sister's grave. I prefer to go there by myself. Usually it's pretty quiet and peaceful. Since I live 2,000 miles away, I am not able to go often, but I treasure the times I can be in such a quiet place.

Standing in the cemetery more than 20 years ago, I grew up in hurry. For a long time it was a bitter reminder of what had been lost. Now it's a place where I'm reminded of what was gained.

I was at college getting ready for finals when a call came late one Saturday night with the news that my sister had been killed in an automobile accident. A drunk driver had hit her head-on. She was 18—a senior in high school. All her plans and dreams were gone in an instant. A few days before Christmas we buried my sister Darcy.

Lots of things seemed lost at the time. My parents lost their joy. Her friends lost a great confidant. The world lost a very good person. I lost a naïve belief that life would always be good. In that cemetery more than a lifeless body was buried.

It has been said time heals all wounds and maybe it does. At the very least it gives you a different perspective. When I stand beside her grave, I am still saddened by the loss, and I often wonder what kind of life Darcy would have had. I wonder what our relationship would be like. Would we still be close? I have to work hard to recall the sound of her voice or the smile on her face. When I go there now I am reminded of how fragile life is, how valuable each moment is, how much we need our friends, and how great a difference faith and hope make.

There is much that has been gained since that day when so much was lost. More than anything else, hope has been gained. Hope that I will see Darcy again. Hope that death is never the final word.

My sister was a Christian, and the summer before her death she had grown considerably in her Christian faith, learning to dance joyfully in her heavenly father's embrace. On the day of her death she was a bridesmaid in a friend's wedding. At the reception she danced with my father. And I believe, because of her faith, that very night she danced in a whole new way with the Father in Heaven.

On the stone that marks her grave are these words:

> *Grieve not for me,*
> *Nor let one small tear fall.*
> *For what you can only dream,*
> *I can see. And friend*
> *'Tis worth it all, 'tis worth it all.*

—Rick Rusaw

Whom have you lost to death? What do you miss most about them?

_____

_____

_____

_____

_____

_____

_____

_____

_____

_____

_____

_____

What do you picture your loved ones doing, right now, in Heaven? What are you most looking forward to about seeing them again one day?

The Greatest Failure

"I will not leave you as orphans; I will come to you."

JOHN 14:18

THE GREATEST FAILURE

He was one of the biggest failures of all time. He failed over and over again. With one invention he failed 10,000 times before he was successful. And yet he was perhaps the world's greatest inventor, Thomas Alva Edison.

Edison is the definition of tenacity. His focused mind and dogged determination led to electric lighting, the phonograph, and the motion picture camera. We are all grateful that he had the confidence and the drive to overcome his thousands of failures to finally arrive at each hard-earned success.

Our world is truly a better place because of Edison. His drive to succeed is an example for us to press on in the face of seemingly insurmountable obstacles. But as successful as he was in overcoming his failures as an inventor, there was one kind of failure Thomas Edison never overcame. Edison was a failure as a father and husband.

Edison's first wife, along with his three children, rarely saw him. His wife was so lonely that many think it was the reason for the severe illness that led to her death at the age of 29. Edison's first three children were emotionally crippled by their father's absence. Thomas Edison, Jr., interpreted his father's rejection as his own failure, and he died a broken alcoholic.

I don't know what drove Thomas Edison or whose esteem he sought, but imagine what would have happened in his family if he had been as driven by love as he was by invention.

Psalm 27:10 says, "Though my father and mother forsake me, the LORD will receive me." Maybe you've felt like a failure, like an experiment gone wrong. Maybe you feel like the son of Thomas Edison, abandoned by those you love. I encourage you, no matter how tough it seems, don't give up. Don't lose hope. The one who made Thomas Edison is still working on you, and he never fails.

—*Dan Stuecher*

In what ways do you feel like a failure? By whom do you feel abandoned?

_____

_____

_____

_____

_____

_____

_____

_____

_____

_____

_____

_____

_____

How does knowing that God will always love you and that he's
not finished with you yet help you with your feelings of failure
and abandonment?

_____

_____

_____

_____

_____

_____

_____

_____

_____

_____

_____

_____

Luther Luckett

The scroll of the prophet Isaiah was handed to him [Jesus].

Unrolling it, he found the place where it is written:

"The Spirit of the Lord is on me,

> *because he has anointed me*

> *to preach good news to the poor.*

He has sent me to proclaim freedom for the prisoners

> *and recovery of sight for the blind,*

to release the oppressed,

> *to proclaim the year of the Lord's favor."*

Then he rolled up the scroll, gave it back to the attendant and sat down. The eyes of everyone in the synagogue were fastened on him, and he began by saying to them, "Today this scripture is fulfilled in your hearing."

LUKE 4:17–21

LUTHER LUCKETT

I was really anxious about my first visit. I'm talking about my first visit to an inmate in a prison. I didn't know what to expect, what to say, or what to do. But my fear didn't keep me away, and what I learned was worth the visit.

It was called Luther Luckett Correctional Institute. Though I was afraid of the unknown, I really wanted to visit Adam, a friend of mine who was serving time for a crime he admits he committed. I drove to the prison, went through all the proper inspections, handed over everything but my clothes, and signed papers confirming my visit. I was led to a large room that looked like a school cafeteria—a lot of tables and chairs, a lot of guests, and a lot of prisoners. This was obviously a low security area for non-violent offenders. In walked Adam. He looked just the way he always had. He had a look of peace on his face—it was faint but, nonetheless, it was there. We sat and talked, and then Adam went back to his cell and I collected my belongings and went home.

While visiting Adam in that prison I learned that inmates are people. They may have committed crimes, but they haven't lost their humanity. Adam was at peace with God because he'd confessed his guilt. He was also at peace with himself because he didn't have to hide or lie about his crime. Though in prison, Adam was free. And Adam knew that he was loved—loved by a God who looks beyond the past and offers a future of hope. Adam helped me see that hope, not just for him, but for me as well. It is a hope that knows no boundaries or bars, a hope that blooms beyond the walls of our failures. It is a hope in the boundless love of Jesus Christ.

I'm glad I visited Adam in prison. I didn't know I would find so much hope there.

—*Greg Allen*

In what ways do you feel like a prisoner in your life? What is keeping you "chained up"?

Look in the back of your Bible, or in a concordance, for all the verses about freedom. In your own words, write out two or three of your favorites.

Write out a prayer, asking God for hope and for freedom from the things that are holding you prisoner.

_____

_____

_____

_____

_____

_____

_____

_____

_____

_____

_____

_____

_____

The Dance

The angel showed me the river of the water of life, as clear as crystal, flowing from the throne of God and of the Lamb down the middle of the great street of the city. On each side of the river stood the tree of life, bearing twelve crops of fruit, yielding its fruit every month. And the leaves of the tree are for the healing of the nations. No longer will there be any curse. The throne of God and of the Lamb will be in the city, and his servants will serve him. They will see his face, and his name will be on their foreheads. There will be no more night. They will not need the light of a lamp or the light of the sun, for the Lord God will give them light. And they will reign for ever and ever.

REVELATION 22:1–5

THE DANCE

Out of the poor neighborhoods and taverns, a kind of music was born that had such a wild rhythm it sent people into a whirling frenzy. Young men and women moved to the beat in ways that were considered indecent, inappropriate, and just plain wrong. Critics called this "dancing" an epidemic.

The dancing was the brainchild of a single musician who set the world on fire with his particular brand of entertainment, turning out one hit after another. No, I'm not talking about Elvis Presley. This musician lived 100 years earlier, and his music was made popular in Vienna, Austria. The musician was Johann Strauss (the younger), and the wild dancing was none other than the waltz.

> *Danube so blue*
> *As onward you flow*
> *My heart is with you*
> *Wherever you go.*

Those are the words to the most famous composition by Strauss— *The Blue Danube* waltz. The music and the words fit well with the character of Strauss, who was engaged to be married 12 times in his life. He was not a philanderer but, rather, someone who was forever longing for the perfect love. Strauss was a romantic, the kind of person who could see blue in what was, without question, a very gray Danube River. When he was 37, Strauss finally found his soul mate and true love, and they were married. Tragically, his wife died just a few years later.

Like Strauss, we are all surrounded by tragedy in a fallen world, yet we do not anticipate its inevitability in our lives. We dance the dance of desire and try to create a Heaven on Earth that is as much an apparition as the blueness of the Danube.

Strauss learned that there is no perfect love, that life is full of suffering, and that the Danube River isn't blue. But that is not the end of the story. While this world may be full of heartache, there is hope—the hope of Heaven, where all rivers do run blue, where all loves are soul mates, and where the waltz goes on all night long. Strauss lived in a time when people lingered over thoughts of Heaven, looking forward to the welcoming embrace of our loving Father. He lived in a time when people thought of eternity not as wishful thinking but as the reality that exists on the other side of time and space. And, in spite of the hardships life brings our way, that vision of Heaven can be enough to keep our dance going all night long.

—Eric Snyder for Paul S. Williams

What is your vision of Heaven? Write down some of your ideas of what it is like. How does this vision make you feel?

When you think about Heaven, knowing that you will be there one day, how does it change your view of life here and now?

_____

_____

_____

_____

_____

_____

_____

_____

_____

_____

_____

_____

_____

_____

A Speck, and Then . . .

Brothers, we do not want you to be ignorant about those who fall
asleep, or to grieve like the rest of men, who have no hope.
We believe that Jesus died and rose again and so we believe that
God will bring with Jesus those who have fallen asleep in him. . . .
For the Lord himself will come down from heaven, with a loud
command, with the voice of the archangel and with the trumpet
call of God, and the dead in Christ will rise first. After that, we
who are still alive and are left will be caught up together with
them in the clouds to meet the Lord in the air. And so we will be
with the Lord forever.

1 THESSALONIANS 4:13, 14, 16, 17

A SPECK, AND THEN . . .

My three children suffered terribly when one of their close friends was killed in an automobile accident. The life of their friend was celebrated in a memorial service that included the telling of bittersweet stories of their shared lives, what was and is now gone. My children and their friends were having a tough time. It was the first time they had been so closely touched by death. I felt badly when I had to leave town just one day later.

I told my children I would return in a few days and we would talk again. Then I drove down Marilyn Street with misty eyes. As I headed to the airport my thoughts were with my children in their grieving. It is a difficult thing to be a father and have no special magic to make things better.

Deep in thought, I arrived at the airport, barely noticing as a 737 taxied onto runway 24 and took off to the south. I'd seen similar scenes thousands of times. But for some reason, I looked up and watched the jet circle high above the airport, then make a beeline for the skies above the Great South Bay and the open Atlantic. Before long it was only a speck in the distance, and then it was gone.

That is how the week felt for my children. A good friend, ready to challenge life with power to spare, was gone, and now he was slowly disappearing from view. They wanted to keep him in their hearts, but they didn't know how.

As I waited for my flight to depart, all I could think of was their grief. And then I thought again of that jet, and how it had disappeared across the Atlantic. I looked at my watch and realized the same jet was now preparing to land in Baltimore. I imagined just one person in Baltimore waiting for that flight, searching the evening sky for just a speck of light, knowing their loved one was inside. Then I pictured the outline of a commercial jetliner with two engines beneath the wings coming into view, and a brightly colored fuselage landing and taxiing to the gate. I imagined the reunion they were about to have when that loved one got off the plane and someone in Maryland got her heart's desire.

It seemed to be a heavenly reminder. Someone is waiting at the other end of the journey.

In my neck of the woods it has not been fashionable to talk about the afterlife for several decades now. As a culture, we're paying the price for it. We may nominally believe in Heaven, but it's not a topic for open discourse. And in the process we lose sight of the hope we have that death is not the final word. We easily dismiss the story of Heaven and the Jesus who has gone ahead to prepare a place for us there.

When I got home from my trip, but before I was fully through the front door, I gave a long hug to my children. And before I even put down my suitcase I said to them, "Whatever you do, when you think of your friend, remember eternity.

"While you were grieving after the funeral, on the other side of time and space a celebration was just commencing. A heavenly host stood just inside the gates, gazing toward the eastern skies. First there was a speck on the horizon, and then unmistakably the outline of a soul, your friend's soul, coming home. And while we lost sight of him in New York, God opened the gates and embraced one of his own, and the angels had a party that went on all night long."

If you can really understand the profound truth of that reality, I told my children, you will grieve, but your grief will be touched with joy.

—*Paul S. Williams*

Have you ever waited on the arrival of a loved one from far away?
How did you feel as you waited? What was it like to finally see
that person again?

_____

_____

_____

_____

_____

_____

_____

_____

_____

_____

_____

_____

_____

Think about someone you've lost to death. What do you think his arrival in Heaven was like? Who was there to greet him? Write out your ideas and impressions of that heavenly homecoming.

_____

_____

_____

_____

_____

_____

_____

_____

_____

_____

_____

_____

_____

Too Much Is at Stake

Let us hold unswervingly to the hope we profess, for he who prom-
ised is faithful. And let us consider how we may spur one another
on toward love and good deeds. Let us not give up meeting
together, as some are in the habit of doing, but let us encourage
one another—and all the more as you see the Day approaching.

HEBREWS 10:23–25

TOO MUCH IS AT STAKE

Often, I do not know how to rest in the love of God. I believe the gospel is true. I believe God is love. I believe God came to Earth as a man, died, and was raised again. I believe that after I die God wants me to live with him on the other side of time and space in a place called Heaven. I believe that. But I have a very difficult time living as if I believe that. Do you feel that way?

My roots are deep in Christianity. I've been attending church services since I was one week old. But as deep as they go, I often find my roots are dry, thirsty, crackling, and parched. For long periods I don't feel the presence of Jesus at all. I go to church. I worship. I pray. But I feel no peace. When confronted with illness and struggle, I only plot my own course, trusting in nothing but my own ingenuity. And it's not enough.

Like the poet Gerard Manley Hopkins, in one of what he called his melancholy sonnets, I pray from the depths of my parched soul, "O thou Lord of life, send my roots rain."

In one of the darkest times of my life, I found myself on the out-skirts of Vienna, in a place called the Stift, a Cistercian monastery that has been there since 1158. Every evening while I was teaching at a seminary nearby, I went to compline, and I listened, night after night, as the psalms were sung in Latin, just as they have been sung every night for over 800 years. And listening to that plainsong, the sounds of the brothers' voices ringing off the Romanesque and Gothic walls, I knew the truth: that there is only one way to water a thirsty soul, and that is to come and drink at a place of worship, where fellow travelers speak words for the ages and rain falls to the deep places where the roots cry out.

The spiritual journey is no place for lone souls. This is meant to be a communal journey, traveled with fellow pilgrims. I once was living in my head, as I am prone to do, and a fellow traveler took her hand and placed it on my stomach and said to me, "Stay here, in your gut, near your heart, and you will hear the voice of God." And that hand on my stomach brought rain. Just like the psalms sung in Vienna every night bring rain.

So don't navigate this hazardous journey alone. Too much is at stake.

—Paul S. Williams

Who has helped you in your times of sorrow and struggle? What specific things did they do or say that comforted and encouraged you?

Whom do you know that could use your comfort and encouragement? What specific, practical things can you do to help them in their struggle?

The Mother of All Prayers

I pray also that the eyes of your heart may be enlightened in order that you may know the hope to which he has called you, the riches of his glorious inheritance in the saints, and his incomparably great power for us who believe.

EPHESIANS 1:18, 19

THE MOTHER OF ALL PRAYERS

Monica had a bad son. She was a good mother and a devout woman, but her son was a holy terror. She read Scripture to him and prayed for him daily, but it was to no avail. By the time he was 16 he was a thief and a drunk. By the age of 18 he had fathered an illegitimate child. To his mother's shame, his life was characterized by a series of illicit affairs, prostitutes, and orgies. It would have been understandable if Monica had given up on her son. Instead, Monica prayed.

For years she prayed for her wayward son. Little changed. Her son did become a lawyer, but it was only to earn enough money to continue his self-centered lifestyle. It seemed Monica's prayers were all in vain. But her son knew differently. His mother's faithfulness was a constant irritant. He remembered the things she said to him as a child. It all came back vividly upon the death of one of his close friends. The brevity of life and the hollowness he felt inside began to haunt him. He started an intense search for meaning and truth. All roads seemed to lead to Christ. By his late twenties there was only one thing holding him back—he thought it was impossible for him to escape the slavery of his desires.

His addictions seemed to control his life. And then one day, at the age of 32, alone in a garden, he heard what seemed to be the voice of a child saying, "Take up and read." He ran to find a Bible. When he opened it, his eyes fell on these words from Romans 13:14: "Clothe yourselves with the Lord Jesus Christ, and do not think about how to gratify the desires of the sinful nature." He suddenly realized the first step he had to take was to decide to live like Jesus Christ, loving God and loving others. He then began to understand that first step would make every other step possible. "Instantly," he later wrote, "a light of serenity infused into my heart."

A mother's prayers had been answered. The year was A.D. 386. In time, Monica's son grew in his faith. He eventually became one of the most prolific theologians in the history of the Christian church. His name was Augustine. And he is a reminder to mothers everywhere that God is in the business of making saints out of even the worst of sinners.

—Eric Snyder for Paul S. Williams

Write down the names of some children or young people you know who seem to be heading down the wrong path.

_____

_____

_____

_____

_____

_____

_____

_____

_____

_____

_____

_____

Write a short prayer for each person you listed, lifting up to the
Lord each one's specific needs.

_____

_____

_____

_____

_____

_____

_____

_____

_____

_____

_____

_____

_____

Where Darkness Resides

Many, O LORD my God,

   are the wonders you have done

The things you planned for us

   no one can recount to you;

were I to speak and tell of them,

   they would be too many to declare.

PSALM 40:5

WHERE DARKNESS RESIDES

*"Have the gates of death been shown to you? Have you seen the gates
of the shadow of death? Have you comprehended the vast expanses of
the earth? Tell me, if you know all this. What is the way to the abode
of light? And where does darkness reside? Can you take them to their
places? Do you know the paths to their dwellings?"*

God's words in Job 38:17–20 were not the answers that Job was
expecting. Having suffered so much, he was asking for the
answer to one simple question, "Why?" But he didn't get an
answer—he got more questions. Was Job being left in the dark?

Frank Borman is a man who is familiar with a darkness that Job
could have never known. In 1968, he, along with two other
brave souls, journeyed to the very place where darkness resides,
and in so doing, received an answer to Job's question.

With a whirlwind, God pummeled Job with questions. By con-
trast, God spoke to Frank Borman and his friends, Jim Lovell
and William Anders, from the Sea of Tranquility. These men
were the crew of *Apollo 8*, the first manned mission to the moon.
On Christmas Eve, 1968, they entered lunar orbit and beheld the
darkness that human eyes had never seen, the backside of the
moon. As they completed the first of 10 orbits they described
what they saw as a "vast loneliness" an indescribable "bleakness";
and then, suddenly, the men were awestruck. The earth, more
beautiful than they had imagined, began to rise just above the
moon's horizon. Commander Borman and his crew captured
the image live. The world was looking at "the world" for the first
time. It was also listening. Borman was asked to have his crew
say something to honor the event. From the heavens to the earth
the three men delivered their answer to Job's "why?"

From our perspective the earth may sometimes seem like a vast loneliness, tilted on an axis of suffering and despair. So what would the *Apollo 8* crew say to a world of people looking to the heavens with a collective "Why?" With a voice full of emotion, Pilot William Anders began:

"For all the people on Earth, the crew of *Apollo 8* has a message we would like to send you:

"In the beginning God created the heaven and the earth.

And the earth was without form, and void; and darkness was upon the face of the deep.

And the Spirit of God moved upon the face of the waters. And God said, Let there be light: and there was light. And God saw the light, that it was good: and God divided the light from the darkness." (KJV)

All three astronauts read aloud from Genesis 1, and as they sent us a picture of an earth firmly on its axis, for a moment at least, they changed all of our "whys" to wonder.

—*Paul S. Williams*

What circumstances in your life have caused you to ask "why"?
Did you ever receive an answer?

_____

_____

_____

_____

_____

_____

_____

_____

_____

_____

_____

_____

_____

Now, think of things that cause you to stand in wonder. List as many as you can. How can these things quiet your "why" questions?

Full of Life

Be at rest once more, O my soul,

for the LORD has been good to you.

For you, O LORD, have delivered my soul from death,

my eyes from tears,

my feet from stumbling,

that I may walk before the LORD

in the land of the living.

PSALM 116:7–9

FULL OF LIFE

Her grandson said of her, "Yes, she's an older woman, but she is so full of life." Throughout her life she has faced hardship and disappointment. Her childhood home was incredibly unstable, and her adult life has been marked by tragedy. Yet somehow, through incredible pain, she has found grace. A grace that seeped up through the hard splintered floor of life to touch her soul in the kind of way that makes her own grandchildren say she's "full of life." What is the source of that marvelous grace?

At the age of four her mother left her with neighbors and took off for several months. That was just the first abandonment in a pattern that continued for years. Her happiest childhood moments were the periods of time she spent in foster care with a loving family.

Her hardships didn't end with childhood though. She married right out of high school and quickly had two children. A third child died shortly after birth. A fourth died during childbirth, and a fifth she had to carry a few weeks before delivery, already knowing the baby was dead.

When her daughter was 18 a police officer showed up at her door to tell her their beautiful girl had been killed by a drunk driver. "I guess God doesn't want me to be a mother," she said in those dark hours. Six months later her best friend died. Two weeks after that her mother, with whom she had reconciled, also died. It was the worst time of her life. Yet in the midst of all this unspeakable heartache, God's grace was sufficient, and she remained "full of life."

She was abandoned and abused as a child. She lost four of her own children. She has seen the darkest moments of grief up close and personal. Yet she still retains a soft heart and a life filled with . . . well, life. Recently a lifelong friend wrote and asked, "How have you done it? How have you survived all of this tragedy? Is it your faith? Your friends?" She would answer that it has been her faith *and* her friends. God has sustained her and her friends have supported her. Those who know her say that she gained by giving. Somehow, early in life, she came to see that through giving to others, her own wounds would be healed.

Throughout her life she has provided grace, acceptance, love, and compassion to others who have lived the same tragic stories she has known. She has helped them through grief and lifted them through hopelessness. She has prayed and cried with them as they moved through life's darkest hours. Hers is a story of hope—hope in God, hope in life, hope that is seen in the way she lives. Her grandchildren are right. She is an inspiration to many—and to no one more than to me. I know, because I'm talking about the person who gave me hope and courage for my journey. I'm talking about my mom.

—*Rick Rusaw*

Do you know people who are "full of life"? Do you know the circumstances of their lives? Take time to talk with them about their struggles and ask how they stay joyful in spite of those struggles.

What struggles have taken some of the life out of you? Ask God to give you his joy in spite of them, so that you too may be called "full of life"!

Morning Will Come

Weeping may remain for a night,

but rejoicing comes in the morning.

PSALM 30:5

MORNING WILL COME

They met in the spring under a blooming jacaranda tree. Will was the neighborhood paperboy. Every dawn he sleepily tossed the concerns of the world onto the lawns of a small southern town. Joy was 12 then. She would wake before the sun and peer through the dangling Spanish moss to catch a glimpse of Will on his red bicycle. One morning Will saw the sun rise upon her face as if it had been waiting since creation for that very moment. Right then and there he prayed to the God of his childhood that he would behold that face for the rest of his days.

Seventy years from that moment the sun finally set. A harsh wind pierced Will's bones as he stood before an icy grave freshly carved from a snow-covered plot. They picked this spot together, he and Joy, never knowing who would be the first to occupy it. The gray sky turned black as Joy's body was lowered into the ground.

Will's feeble legs carried him to the tiny northern house he and Joy had called home. The two-bedroom Cape Cod felt like a mausoleum. As he unlocked the door he noticed the large clay pots scattered along the porch. Joy had tried many times to nurse a jacaranda tree, but it wasn't suited for the northern climate.

In the corner of the guest room sat the one object that had nearly destroyed them both—a small, white bassinette, now draped with scarves. It had never been filled with anything but pain. The baby was stillborn, a girl. It was then that Will stopped worshiping the God of his childhood and pondered an unknown God, much darker than he had envisioned.

Still, every morning Joy would put on a pot of coffee as Will sat at the kitchen table and read aloud from the Scriptures. In their grief the Scriptures had a different meaning. And the prayers had a different tone. But after a long, cold winter, their hearts finally warmed again.

Night had fallen on the little house now. The silence made Joy's absence especially keen. Will longed desperately to feel her near him.

Will rose from his bed before dawn the next day accompanied only by the pain in his feeble legs and the familiar ache of his heart. He dressed, went to the kitchen, and put on a pot of coffee. He sat at the table and read aloud from the Scriptures. He knew that whatever the condition of the previous night, the light eventually came with the morning. And sometimes, on the most difficult mornings, it comes bearing a gift. At the right moment the God of Will's childhood joys and his present sorrows touched him with comfort.

Deep in his heart, Will could hear God whisper, "She is with me, and I am with you. You are not alone." Night had come, but Will was sure that the morning would dawn again and that one day he and Joy would stand beneath the jacaranda tree once again—together—in eternity.

—*Eric Snyder for Paul S. Williams*

What dark nights have you been through? Are you still going through a dark and lonely time? Pour out your sadness to the Lord in writing.

_____

_____

_____

_____

_____

_____

_____

_____

_____

_____

_____

_____

_____

_____

Remember that God promises to bring you light once again.
Write out your longings for that dawn—a prayer of faith that God
will bring the morning again.

_____

_____

_____

_____

_____

_____

_____

_____

_____

_____

_____

_____

_____

Through Locked Doors

*On the evening of that first day of the week, when the disciples
were together, with the doors locked for fear of the Jews, Jesus came
and stood among them and said, "Peace be with you!" After he
said this, he showed them his hands and side. The disciples were
overjoyed when they saw the Lord.*

JOHN 20:19, 20

THROUGH LOCKED DOORS

Some years ago an acquaintance of mine took his own life. It was a very sad time for all of us who knew him. He was kind, fun-loving, insightful—a good man. Many people encouraged and supported him, but the wounds of life were too deep, and he succumbed to the darkness on a warm summer night along the white sands of the east coast. As strong as love can be, sometimes it stands helpless at a door that has no outside handle and can only be opened from the inside.

There are two interesting stories in the Gospels of Jesus' life after his resurrection. On the Sunday night of resurrection day, his disciples were meeting together in a room when all of a sudden, through a bolted door, here came Jesus. Since childhood that image captured me. Jesus entered through a bolted door.

Eight days later on a Monday night he did it again. Two times, in the midst of crisis and turmoil, when the world had been turned upside down, Jesus came in through a bolted door. And that is where my hope lies.

There is a famous painting by Holman Hunt called *The Christ Who Knocks.* You may have seen it before. A kind and loving Jesus, with a lantern in his hand, stands at a door and knocks. But the door has no handle on the outside. The implication is that Jesus can only help if the person inside turns the handle to let him in.

But I'm not so sure about that image. It is the same Jesus who walked through two locked doors—walked in to encourage scared men with wounded souls, men who were utterly without hope.

There have been dark nights of the soul when I have removed the outside handles on the doors of my heart. I've kept the doors locked, keeping myself from others simply by refusing to open the door from the inside. But in the midst of those times of darkness and despair, this one thing I have learned to be true. There is a God who walks through locked doors to heal wounded hearts.

145

—*Paul S. Williams*

What in your life has caused you to lock the doors of your heart and soul? Why?

_____

_____

_____

_____

_____

_____

_____

_____

_____

_____

_____

_____

_____

_____

Write a prayer, being completely honest with God about how you feel and about why you have locked yourself away. He will meet you behind the locked door.

_____

_____

_____

_____

_____

_____

_____

_____

_____

_____

_____

_____

_____

Joe Kemper

We know that in all things God works for the good of those who love him, who have been called according to his purpose.

ROMANS 8:28

JOE KEMPER

You'd really like Joe Kemper. He's a gentle man in his eighties who still walks three miles a day, smiles at everyone who crosses his path, and volunteers every day at his church. If it were ever your pleasure to have done anything for Joe, you would know he never forgets it, because he thanks you every time he sees you. Joe often takes people to lunch, his treat. And then he tells them how good God has been to him.

And what makes all that even more remarkable is that Joe has known terrible tragedy. His wife was killed in a car accident. His grandson took his own life. He has had numerous surgeries himself. It would be no surprise if Joe said to God, "If this is the way you treat your friends, it's no wonder you have so many enemies."

But that's not Joe.

Joe Kemper lost a wife, a grandson, and his own health. Yet he still celebrates how good God has been to him. Joe understands that God does not promise an end to suffering on this side of life. Instead, God sent his own Son to suffer alongside us—to know the pain we know when a loved one dies, to understand the grief of a young life cut short by a tragic decision, to know the importance of moving on through pain to another dawn.

And Joe understands that sometimes our suffering here is compounded by not thinking enough about eternity. My 3-year-old daughter gets mighty upset when I don't let her have candy before dinner. All she can think of is the moment and that candy. She doesn't understand that I see the bigger picture—that there's a meal coming that will satisfy her hunger far better than a little bit of candy.

And so it is with Joe. He suffers now, but he triumphs over his suffering, because he knows a marvelous meal is coming—a feast that will satisfy his hunger forever.

Joe Kemper is a special friend to God. And although we would call the terrible things that happened to Joe tragedies, the question is whether or not God is in the tragedies. I believe that God is not only in the tragedies, but that he will take those tragedies and stand them on their heads once we get to Heaven. That's why Joe volunteers at his church every single day. That's why he is constantly thanking others for their kindnesses. That is why he is constantly encouraging others along the way. Because Joe Kemper knows God is in the midst of every tragedy. And that even in those tragedies, if we'll only reach out to him, his love will be enough to get us through to the joy on the other side.

—Greg Allen

151

Read the story of another "Joe" in Genesis 37, 39–41. What are the tragedies he faced? How did he deal with them?

_____

_____

_____

_____

_____

_____

_____

_____

_____

_____

_____

_____

_____

_____

List some of the specific lessons you have learned from both
Joes about how to have joy in the midst of difficulties.

_____

_____

_____

_____

_____

_____

_____

_____

_____

_____

_____

_____

_____

It Was So Dark

Mary stood outside the tomb crying. As she wept, she bent over to look into the tomb and saw two angels in white, seated where Jesus' body had been, one at the head and the other at the foot. They asked her, "Woman, why are you crying?"

"They have taken my Lord away," she said, "and I don't know where they have put him." At this, she turned around and saw Jesus standing there, but she did not realize that it was Jesus. "Woman," he said, "why are you crying? Who is it you are looking for?"

Thinking he was the gardener, she said, "Sir, if you have carried him away, tell me where you have put him, and I will get him." Jesus said to her, "Mary." . . . Mary Magdalene went to the disciples with the news: "I have seen the Lord!"

JOHN 20:11–18

IT WAS SO DARK

It was so dark. There were rain, howls, haunting cries of desperation and betrayal—the cries of a mother over the death of her child. Jesus was dead. The world had come to a complete stop, and the sun was black. It was so dark.

And yet, it was Easter. We usually think of Easter as white, bright, joyful. And we should. Easter exists because Jesus defeated death. But Easter Sunday didn't start out with lilies and laughter. On that first Easter morning, when Mary went to the tomb where Jesus had been buried, it was dark. Though it was morning, the sun hadn't yet lit the day. And though Jesus wasn't in the tomb, Mary hadn't assumed he was alive. She thought his body had been stolen. The Son of God had been bodily raised from the dead by God, his Father, but Mary didn't know it. To her it was still so dark.

When Mary Magdalene found Jesus' tomb empty in the dark of that first Easter morning, she told the disciples. John and Peter ran to the tomb. Mary was right. There was no Jesus. Just the linens used for the burial. Empty linens. And when they saw that, John and Peter believed—they believed Jesus had risen from the dead. They didn't understand it, but they believed it.

Many people are just like those friends of Jesus. They don't fully understand why God would have his Son live with us, love us, heal us, die for us, and be raised from the dead to offer us hope. But they believe it. And that is called faith. It's the distinguishing mark of Christians. On Easter morning, faith is what causes me to celebrate an empty tomb and worship a risen Lord.

Now, although Peter and John may have had faith that Jesus had risen from the dead, Mary was still in the dark, weeping, believing her Lord had been killed and his body now stolen. But as she wept, a man asked Mary why she was crying. Mary thought he was just a gardener, another early riser who was going about a normal day's work. But there was nothing normal about this man or this encounter. Mary recognized his voice, and turning toward him, she recognized him. It was Jesus. He was alive. And he privileged Mary with a personal visit. She saw, and she believed.

But for the rest of us, this Easter we must believe without seeing. We will read the story from Scripture and we have to choose to believe. Once again that is called faith. And faith is what makes Easter real for all of us who live this side of that first Easter. Faith is what turns dark into light. And faith leads to hope and trust and joy and life—for all eternity!

—*Greg Allen*

What does Easter mean to you? Is it just a time to celebrate spring? Or is it truly the celebration of Jesus' triumph over death?

_____

_____

_____

_____

_____

_____

_____

_____

_____

_____

_____

_____

_____

Write a prayer asking God to make the story of Easter real to you. Ask him to open your eyes to recognize who he really is, just as Mary's eyes were finally opened at the empty tomb.

_____

_____

_____

_____

_____

_____

_____

_____

_____

_____

_____

_____

_____

_____

Grandpa Bell

Children's children are a crown to the aged.

proverbs 17:6

We will not hide them from their children;

we will tell the next generation

the praiseworthy deeds of the Lord,

his power, and the wonders he has done.

psalm 78:4

GRANDPA BELL

Every summer my parents drove me to Big Clifty, Kentucky. It was just down the road from Little Clifty. My grandparents had a farm there, fully equipped with a little white house and big red barn. There were 66 acres for a boy to discover. There was a great "holler," the country name for a valley with a creek at the bottom. I'd take many an expedition to the bottom of that "holler" with King, my grandparents' big collie.

Without question my favorite memories of Big Clifty are those times Grandpa Bell said, "Hey, boy, wanna go feed the cows?" Grandpa's cows were big, to me at least. Grandpa knew all the cows by name. Old Bessie always seemed to be watching me. She had a bell around her neck. I was glad; that meant I could hear if she was sneaking up on me. But I was really never worried, not as long as I was with Grandpa Bell.

When I was 10 Grandpa and I were walking down the lane to feed Old Bessie and the rest of the cattle, and Grandpa pulled out his chewing tobacco. I asked him for a pinch. He said, "Your momma wouldn't be happy with me, boy."

"Oh, Grandpa, I'll never tell her," I promised.

"Your grandma wouldn't be happy either," he said.

"Oh come on, Grandpa, just a little pinch," I begged.

With a mischievous twinkle in his eye, he pinched off a little of that tobacco twist and told me to be sure not to bite it, just to let it rest between my cheek and gum. Of course I couldn't resist, and I bit into it. Five seconds later my mouth was on fire. Five more seconds and I spit the whole wad out of my mouth. I cried a little; Grandpa laughed a lot.

I always loved being with Grandpa Bell. And then, suddenly one summer, it happened. I noticed there was something different. Grandpa didn't seem himself. He had had a stroke. I didn't know what a stroke was; I just knew that Grandpa changed. Before long he was in a nursing home. I was shocked when I first visited him there. My really big grandpa was not much bigger than I. No more feeding Old Bessie or walks down the lane.

Grandpa died after I graduated from college. I cried at the funeral. He was the greatest. Every now and again I still cry when I think of him. I'd love for my three daughters to have met Grandpa. They would have loved him. So, I do what every dad should do—I tell my children wonderful stories about Grandpa Bell and watch their faces twinkle with the same smile he brought to mine.

163

—*Greg Allen*

Who are the people that bring you a smile when you remember them? What about them brings such great memories?

_____

_____

_____

_____

_____

_____

_____

_____

_____

_____

_____

_____

_____

_____

Write down a few of your favorite memories so you can share them with those you love. Thank God for the gift of those precious memories.

_____

_____

_____

_____

165

_____

_____

_____

_____

_____

_____

_____

_____

Mary and Martha

Jesus said to her, "I am the resurrection and the life. He who

believes in me will live, even though he dies; and whoever lives

and believes in me will never die."

JOHN 11:25, 26

MARY AND MARTHA

Mary and Martha were sisters who had an extremely sick brother named Lazarus. The sisters came to Jesus and told him their brother would surely die unless Jesus came to heal him. With his reputation, you'd think Jesus would have gone right away, but he didn't. Jesus told the sisters to go on home and he'd come later.

Their questions erupted like a violent volcano. Didn't Jesus care? Didn't he want to heal Lazarus? Where was the hope in the face of sure death?

Lazarus had been dead four days when Jesus approached their home. Mary and Martha came running to Jesus with confusion, anger, and a severe lack of hope. Their brother Lazarus was dead. Martha accused Jesus, "If you had been here when we told you, Lazarus wouldn't have died."

That's probably what I would have done. Jesus had a message of love and healing, didn't he? But both seemed absent now.

Jesus had Mary and Martha lead him to the tomb where Lazarus was buried. Jesus cried. It probably made them angry. "Yeah, cry now. If you'd been here in time, there would be nothing to cry about." But Jesus asked them to remove the stone from the tomb. Lazarus had been dead four days—there would surely be a terrible odor. Didn't Jesus realize that? But he asked that the door be opened, and they opened it. And Jesus calmed their fury and restored their hope when he called out "Lazarus," and the dead man walked out.

Jesus hadn't done exactly what they'd asked him to do, but they sure weren't complaining. Hope really did live. But you know, some years later Lazarus died again, just like all of us will someday.

Yes, Lazarus died, but Jesus brought him back to life. And Jesus also died, but God the Father brought him back to life. For all of us who believe and trust in this Jesus, even though we will indeed die, God will raise us to live forever too. And everyone who chooses to believe and live by this basic truth lives with hope that doesn't die.

169

—*Greg Allen*

How would you have felt if you were Mary or Martha? What might you have said to Jesus when he finally arrived?

_____

_____

_____

_____

_____

_____

_____

_____

_____

_____

_____

_____

_____

Have you ever felt that God didn't act quickly enough in a situation in your life? How does the story of Lazarus give you a different perspective on that circumstance?

_____

_____

_____

_____

_____

171

_____

_____

_____

_____

_____

_____

_____

_____

_____

The Love of a Mother

As a mother comforts her child,

so will I comfort you.

ISAIAH 66:13

THE LOVE OF A MOTHER

Mother's Day—it is the holiday that generates more phone calls than any other. More cards are purchased for this day than for any other special occasion. There is and always has been a special bond with between moms and kids. We watch star athletes mouth the words "Mom, I love you" into the camera. There's rarely a message to dad, children, or spouses. It's mom who gets the attention. What is it about mothers that creates such strong connections? Why the heartfelt emotion when it comes to mom?

Just about everyone celebrates Mother's Day. After all, mom was the person who counted toes and recorded memories of nearly every event in our lives. Mom was the early nurturer who can recount our first smiles, first steps, and first words. It was mom we ran to when we were hurt or lonely or afraid. It was mom who loved us in spite of ourselves and provided direction for our journey. No wonder there is such powerful emotion when it comes to moms.

But Mother's Day isn't always an easy day. Maybe you can't be with your mom or your children. Or maybe you've wanted to have children and are unable. Maybe you lost a child or lost your mom. Maybe the relationship with your mom or your kids is a difficult and disappointing one, and Mother's Day is a painful reminder of that. For some of us, Mother's Day isn't an easy day to celebrate. But remember that God hasn't left you alone—even on this day.

We almost always refer to God as our Father, but what about those parts of God we more often equate with motherhood? He's also the God who cares for us, who has recorded every event of our lives, who knows us and loves us in spite of ourselves. He's the God who wants to be the one we turn to when we are hurt, lonely, or afraid. He's the God who can nurture us and provide direction for our journey. Regardless of what Mother's Day brings for you, remember that today and every day God desires to be your father and mother, to hold you in his arms and remind you how deeply you are loved.

—Greg Allen

List the qualities you associate with a loving mother. Think of as many as you can.

_____

_____

_____

_____

_____

_____

_____

_____

_____

_____

_____

_____

_____

_____

How does it make you feel to think of God exhibiting all of those same "motherly" qualities? Does it give you a different view of God than you had before?

_____

_____

_____

_____

_____

_____

_____

_____

_____

_____

_____

_____

_____

Jairus's Daughter

God so loved the world that he gave his one and only Son, that

whoever believes in him shall not perish but have eternal life.

JOHN 3:16

JAIRUS'S DAUGHTER

Anthony drove down from Columbus and stayed all night at the hospital. Anthony's best friend, Tom, had just found out that his 2-year old son, Taylor, had a brain tumor. It would take a biopsy to see if the tumor was cancerous.

The news came back that the tumor was benign, but it was in the brain stem, meaning they'd have to do chemo to try to destroy it. Tom and his wife, Tammy, will not know if the chemo treatment is affecting the tumor until Taylor is a couple years older.

About a month later Anthony called Tom—not to see how little Taylor was doing—but to share unbearable and unbelievable news. Anthony just found out that his little 4-year old girl, Rachel, had the same kind of brain tumor as Taylor.

Why children? Why brain tumors? Where is the hope for two little children battling life's ultimate enemy? I can tell you today that Tom and Tammy, Anthony and Rhonda have hope, but it's not in the chemo. Their ultimate hope is in a man, the same man in whom Jairus found hope.

Jairus lived a long time ago. He, too, had a little child, a daughter, who was dying. But he had hope beyond medicine or doctors. He had hope in a specific man he had seen actually heal people. So Jairus asked the man to heal his daughter. But as they walked up to the door they were met by family members who told them she was already dead. Jairus's friend asked to see the little girl. He whispered a couple of words over her, and then said, "Little girl, get up." And she did.

Jairus's friend is the same friend of Tom and Tammy, Anthony and Rhonda. He is Jesus. Even before Jesus raised Jairus's daughter from the dead, Jarius had hoped Jesus could do just that. And even though Taylor and Rachel are going through chemotherapy at age two and four, their parents are friends with Jesus, and they have hope. I know they do because I've read the e-mail updates and I've heard their words and seen their eyes. But just what kind of hope is this? Even though Jesus raised Jairus's daughter from the dead, she eventually died again. So where is the hope?

The hope is not in this life, but in Jesus himself. Not hope that Jesus will protect, even heal their two precious children, but hope in Jesus. Jesus said that *he* was life and that if we believe in him we will live. Taylor and Rachel's parents have all chosen to find hope in the person of Jesus. If their children live, awesome! But if they should die, Jesus is life.

Please understand, these four parents would be devastated if they lost their children to brain tumors. But they would not mourn as people who have no hope. They believe, as do I, that Jesus is in the business of raising children and adults alike from the dead to live forever. The point is whether or not we will choose to find our hope in this life or in the life of Jesus.

—*Greg Allen*

Read Hebrews 11. While this is called the Faith Hall of Fame it is also about hope. List some of the people mentioned and what they were hoping for during their lives.

Look at Hebrews 11 again. How many people saw their hopes
come true during their lifetimes? How many had to wait until
Heaven to see their hopes fulfilled? How does this give you hope?

_____

_____

_____

_____

_____

_____

_____

_____

_____

_____

_____

_____

■■
Windows of Worship™

Devotions in this book are based on scripts first delivered by Paul Williams and the following hosts for *Worship*.

Greg Allen is a worship minister at Southeast Christian Church in Louisville, Kentucky, where he has served since 1983.

Rick Rusaw is senior minister at LifeBridge Christian Church in Longmont, Colorado, where he has served since 1991.

Dan Stuecher is senior minister at Harborside Christian Church in Safety Harbor, Florida, a congregation he founded in 1984.

Be sure to read and give these other Windows of Worship™ devotional journals.

ISBN 0-7847-1514-9
25001

ISBN 0-7847-1515-7
25002